4/16

RAPTORS!
FALCONS

Emily Wilson

PowerKiDS press™

New York

Published in 2016 by The Rosen Publishing Group, Inc.
29 East 21st Street, New York, NY 10010

First Edition

Editor: Sarah Machajewski
Book Design: Mickey Harmon

Photo Credits: Cover (series logo) Elena Paletskaya/Shutterstock.com; cover, pp. 1, 3–6, 8, 10, 12, 14, 16, 18, 20, 22—24 (border texture; fact box) Picsfive/Shutterstock.com; cover (background scene) silky/Shutterstock.com; cover (falcon flying) Neal Cooper/Shutterstock.com; cover (falcon perched) Chris Hill/Shutterstock.com; p. 5 njaj/Shutterstock.com; p. 7 (main) Phillip Rubino/Shutterstock.com; p. 7 (buzzard) rorue/Shutterstock.com; p. 7 (owl) Alan Tunnicliffe/Shutterstock.com; p. 7 (eagle) Peter Wey/Shutterstock.com; p. 7 (hawk) Volodymyr Burdiak/Shutterstock.com; p. 7 (vulture) Carmine Arienzo/Shutterstock.com; p. 9 © iStockphoto.com/FRANKHILDEBRAND; p. 11 Mohannad Khatib/Shutterstock.com; p. 12 JIM ZIPP/Science Source/Getty Images; p. 13 StockPhotoAstur/Shutterstock.com; p. 15 Sergey Uryadnikov/Shutterstock.com; pp. 17, 18 Alexander Erdbeer/Shutterstock.com; p. 19 Mark Medcalf/Shutterstock.com; p. 21 Mikko HyvÃærinen/Shutterstock.com; p. 22 Tobyphotos/Shutterstock.com.

Cataloging-in-Publication Data

Wilson, Emily.
Falcons / by Emily Wilson.
p. cm. — (Raptors!)
Includes index.
ISBN 978-1-5081-4271-3 (pbk.)
ISBN 978-1-5081-4244-7 (6-pack)
ISBN 978-1-5081-4245-4 (library binding)
1. Falcons — Juvenile literature. I. Wilson, Emily. II. Title.
QL696.F34 W557 2016
598.9'44—d23

Manufactured in the United States of America

CPSIA Compliance Information: Batch #BW16PK: For Further Information contact Rosen Publishing, New York, New York at 1-800-237-9932

Contents

Special Birds

Earth is home to more than 10,000 species, or kinds, of birds. Within that 10,000, there's a group of birds called raptors. Raptors stand apart from other birds because they're skilled hunters. You may have seen one **soaring** through the sky or diving powerfully toward the ground.

Falcons are part of the raptor family. These birds fly at high speeds and use their excellent eyesight to find **prey**. These birds are very special. Read on to find out why.

> This falcon looks like it's getting ready to hunt.

RAPTOR FACTOR

Raptors are also known as birds of prey.

Really Cool Raptors

Raptors are a special group of birds. Not every bird can belong to this group! Birds must have the following features in order to be known as a raptor.

First, raptors are carnivores. That means they only eat meat. Next, raptors must have sharp claws, called talons, as well as good eyesight and hearing. Raptors also have a sharp, hooked beak. These features make raptors some of the best hunters in the world. Falcons have all these features, which is why they're raptors.

Who belongs to the raptor family? This family includes falcons, hawks, eagles, owls, vultures, and buzzards.

eagle

owl

hawk

falcon

vulture

buzzard

7

Falcons Around the World

Falcons belong to a family of animals called Falconidae (fal-KAHN-uh-dee). There are about 60 species of birds in this family, and they're split into two groups. One group is made of falcons, kestrels, and falconets. The other is made of caracaras (kaa-ruh-KAA-ruhz) and forest falcons. This book will focus on the first group.

Falcons are found all over the world. They live on every **continent** except Antarctica. They live in almost every **habitat**, including wooded areas, fields, rocky cliffs, and even cities!

RAPTOR FACTOR

Falcons are so widespread because they migrate. That means they move from one habitat to another based on seasons.

Falcons have no problem making their home near people. Peregrine falcons commonly live on top of tall city buildings.

The Unmistakable Falcon

All raptors have sharp claws, a hooked beak, and great flying abilities. How can you tell a falcon apart from other raptors?

Some raptors are big, but falcons are small to medium sized. Females are usually bigger than males. Falcons are usually a mix of brown, white, black, or gray. Their different-colored feathers make them look spotted or striped.

Falcons have one feature no other raptors have—a **notch** in their beak. This notch creates a bump that acts much like a tooth, and it helps falcons hunt.

RAPTOR FACTOR

Falcon wings are pointy. Other raptors' wings are more rounded.

cone-shaped bone

notched beak

Falcons have tiny cone-shaped bones in their nose openings. They allow a falcon to breathe as it flies at top speeds.

Hunting Habits

Falcons are excellent hunters. They fly very fast and dive at their prey at top speeds. Their way of hunting is different than that of most raptors.

Falcons fly high when they're looking for prey, or they search for it from a **perch**. Some falcon species hover in the air. When falcons spot their prey, they start flying faster. Then, they fold in their wings and dive. Most raptors kill their prey with their claws. Falcons, however, use their beak. They bite through its backbone using their beak notch.

RAPTOR FACTOR

Diving at prey is also called stooping.

The beak notch is an **adaptation** only falcons have. They use it to kill their prey. Then, they use their sharp beak to tear apart its flesh.

Falcon Food

What's the reward for all that hunting? Meat—and lots of it. Some falcon species, such as the peregrine and gyrfalcon, eat smaller birds. They can even catch them midflight.

Most falcons eat small **mammals**, lizards, and bugs. The bat falcon preys on—you guessed it—bats. Like other raptors, some falcons eat carrion, which is the flesh of dead animals.

Even though falcons are near the top of their food chain, they do have their own predators. Falcons are hunted by other raptors, such as owls and eagles.

Falcons don't eat right away—they carry their prey to a different place to eat it. This kestrel chose a tree branch as the place to enjoy a lizard.

The Mighty Peregrine

Peregrine falcons may be the best known of all falcons. They're considered the fastest bird on the planet. They've been known to stoop at more than 200 miles (322 km) per hour!

Peregrine falcons fly thousands of miles a year. If they live in the Arctic and migrate to South America during winter, they may travel more than 15,500 miles (24,945 km) one way.

Not long ago, peregrine falcons were **endangered** because of the harmful effects of **pesticides**. However, people have successfully worked to save them.

RAPTOR FACTOR

Peregrine falcons get their name from a Latin word that means "wanderer."

Peregrine falcons commonly nest in cities. People help keep them safe by not handling or removing their nests.

Nesting and Babies

Falcons commonly make nests on cliffs or in holes in trees. Falcons in cities build nests on top of buildings or bridges. Their nests are often very simple.

Female falcons lay between three and five eggs at a time. The egg color may change based on species, but they're usually white with reddish-brown spots. Baby falcons hatch, or break out of their shell, after about 30 days. Baby falcons can fly after about 35 days.

Peregrine falcons keep the same partner for life. They also return to the same nesting site year after year.

The Ancient Art of Falconry

Falcons are prized for their famous hunting abilities. People have used them to hunt for thousands of years. Falconry is the practice of training a falcon (or other raptor) to hunt. It was a popular sport in ancient China and medieval Europe, and it's still practiced today.

Falconry may seem fun, but it's a lot of work. Falconers spend a lot of time training and raising their birds. They must be responsible and treat their birds with respect. It isn't the same as raising a pet.

RAPTOR FACTOR

States that allow falconry have laws about how to practice the sport. The laws are meant to **protect** both the birds and people.

Falconers wear a special band on their arm to keep the falcon's talons from hurting them. Falcons wear a special hood over their eyes. The hood is thought to keep them calm. When it comes off, the falcon knows it's time to hunt.

Amazing Creatures

Falcons are special creatures. They're different from most birds, including others in the raptor family. They've captured people's attention for thousands of years. Even today, when people see falcons in the wild or in cities, they stop to get a closer look.

Some species of falcons were once in danger of dying out. If this were to happen again, the world would lose something special. If we continue to respect falcons, we can enjoy their company for many years to come.

Glossary

adaptation: A change that helps a living thing survive better in its habitat.

continent: Any of the world's main stretches of land, including Africa, Antarctica, Asia, Australia, Europe, North America, and South America.

endangered: At risk of dying out.

habitat: The natural home of a person, animal, or plant.

mammal: A warm-blooded animal that has a backbone and hair, and feeds milk to its young.

notch: A V-shaped hollow on a falcon's beak that creates a raised point used to kill prey.

perch: A high place on which a bird rests.

pesticide: Matter that's used to kill bugs, but isn't harmful to plants and animals.

prey: An animal that is hunted by another animal for food. Also, to hunt and kill for food.

protect: To keep safe.

soar: To fly or rise high in the air.

Index

Websites

Due to the changing nature of Internet links, PowerKids Press has developed an online list of websites related to the subject of this book. This site is updated regularly. Please use this link to access the list: www.powerkidslinks.com/rapt/falc